Contents

Some words are printed in bold, **like this**. You can find out what they mean on page 30. You can also look in the box at the bottom of the page where they first appear.

Meet the band

A famous rock band is on tour. Millions of fans want to hear them. So the band needs to play in really big places like this sports stadium.

When they start playing, everyone around will hear them. It will be even more exciting for the fans in the stadium. The sound will be so loud that the fans will feel it shaking their whole bodies!

You know who your favourite band is and why you love their music. But how does music – or any sound – actually work? What are sounds made of?

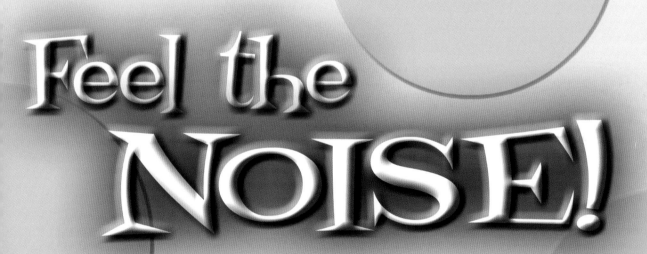

Feel the NOISE!

Anna Claybourne

Raintree

www.raintreepublishers.co.uk

Visit our website to find out more information about **Raintree** books.

To order:
- ☎ Phone 44 (0) 1865 888112
- 🖹 Send a fax to 44 (0) 1865 314091
- 💻 Visit the Raintree bookshop at **www.raintreepublishers.co.uk** to browse our catalogue and order online.

First published in Great Britain by Raintree, Halley Court, Jordan Hill, Oxford OX2 8EJ, part of Harcourt Education.
Raintree is a registered trademark of Harcourt Education Ltd.

© Harcourt Education Ltd 2006
First published in paperback in 2007
The moral right of the proprietor has been asserted.

Editorial: Lucy Thunder and Harriet Milles
Design: Michelle Lisseter, Carolyn Gibson and Bigtop
Illustrations: Darren Lingard
Picture Research: Melissa Allison and Lynda Lines
Production: Camilla Crask

Originated by Dot Gradations Ltd
Printed and bound in Italy by Printer Trento srl

The paper used to print this book comes from sustainable resources.

ISBN 1 844 43851 1 (hardback)
10 09 08 07 06
10 9 8 7 6 5 4 3 2 1

ISBN 1 844 43944 5 (paperback)
10 09 08 07
10 9 8 7 6 5 4 3 2 1

British Library Cataloguing in Publication Data
Claybourne, Anna
Feel the Noise: Sound
534

A full catalogue record for this book is available from the British Library.

Acknowledgements
The publishers would like to thank the following for permission to reproduce photographs: Alamy/ImageState (Robert Llewellyn) pp.20–21; Alamy/Redferns pp. 4–5; Alamy/Rubber Ball Productions pp. 16–17; Alamy/Waring Abbott p. 19 top; Powerstock/mjhunt.com pp. 26–27; Redferns (Phil Dent) pp. 10–11; Rex (Alex Maguire) pp. 8–9; Rex/Mephisto p. 19 bottom; Topfoto (Clive Barda)/PAL pp. 7, 11 inset; Topfoto/Photri p. 25; Topfoto (Talula Sheppard)/Arena PAL pp. 12–13

Cover photograph of a performer singing with a band on stage, reproduced with permission of Lebrecht/Kaloyan Karageorgiev.

The publishers would like to thank Nancy Harris and Harold Pratt for their assistance in the preparation of this book.

Every effort has been made to contact copyright holders of any material reproduced in this book. Any omissions will be rectified in subsequent printings if notice is given to the publishers.

5

Turn the page
to feel the noise!

Setting up

Before a show can start, the band has to test their gear. The drummer starts by hitting a drum to check the sound. A drum is made of a tight skin, or plastic, stretched across the end of a hollow box. When the stick hits the skin, the skin **vibrates**. It moves backwards and forwards many times a second. This makes a sound.

Sound is a type of **energy**. Energy is the ability to do some kind of work. This could be making things move. Sound is made when objects move backwards and forwards, or vibrate. All sounds are caused by vibrating objects.

Sound fact!

A bass drum skin vibrates around 250 times per second.

energy something we use to do work
vibrate to move backwards and forwards quickly

▼ *When a stick hits a drum, it makes a noise. The sound happens because the stick makes the drum skin vibrate.*

7

But how does sound
get to your ears?

Sound check

The band's **sound engineer** checks the instruments. He checks to hear if they are loud enough and if they sound good together. But how does the sound that the band makes get to the sound engineer's ears?

The answer is that sound travels through air. When an object like a drum **vibrates**, it pushes against the air around it. This starts **vibrations** in the air. These are called **sound waves**.

Sound waves spread out through the air and hit other objects. When they hit someone's ears, that person hears the sound.

The sound engineer checks ▶ the sound of the instruments. He checks to hear if they are loud enough, and if they sound good together.

8

sound engineer	sound expert who makes sure bands sound good
sound waves	sound vibrations moving through air
vibrations	fast backwards and forwards movements

Feeling the noise

The band has people called roadies to set up all their gear. While the band is getting ready, the roadies carry things on to the stage. A roadie walks in front of one of the giant speakers. Suddenly a wall of sound hits him.

Have you ever been somewhere really loud? If so, you might have felt sound hitting you, too. In fact, **sound waves** actually do hit you. They make the air move backwards and forwards. If the sound is very loud, the air moves a lot, and you can feel it.

To test this, hold a blown-up balloon against a radio or hi-fi speaker. Your fingers will feel the sound waves making the balloon **vibrate**.

percussion   instruments you play by hitting them

Sound fact!

Evelyn Glennie is deaf, but she is a famous **percussion** player. Evelyn always plays in bare feet. She feels the sound waves with her feet, face, and head.

Ready to rock!

The stadium doors open. The fans rush in to get the best places near the front. The stadium goes dark. Then the stage lights up and the band is on!

A huge cheer goes up as they start to play. The music is so loud that people living nearby can hear it too. Some open their windows so they can get a free concert.

The stage lights go on▶ and the concert starts at last. The band rocks!

Sounds range from very quiet to very loud. You can make sound louder or quieter by using the controls on your radio, TV, or CD player.

So how loud is really loud? Turn the page to find out!

How loud is that?

The loudness of a sound depends on how strong the sound **vibrations** are.

If you hit a drum gently, the skin only moves backwards and forwards and **vibrates** slightly. It sends slight vibrations into the air. If you hit it hard, the vibrations get bigger. The air vibrates more too. The vibrations hit your ears harder, and you hear a louder sound. Loudness is measured in units called **decibels** (dB).

Lawnmower

Traffic

Pin dropping

10 dB 20 dB 30 dB 40 dB 50 dB 60 dB 70 dB 80 dB

Whispering

Talking

Vacuum cleaner

decibel (dB)   measurement of loudness
eardrum   thin skin in the ear that vibrates
                   when sounds reach it
tinnitus   ringing or buzzing sound in the ears

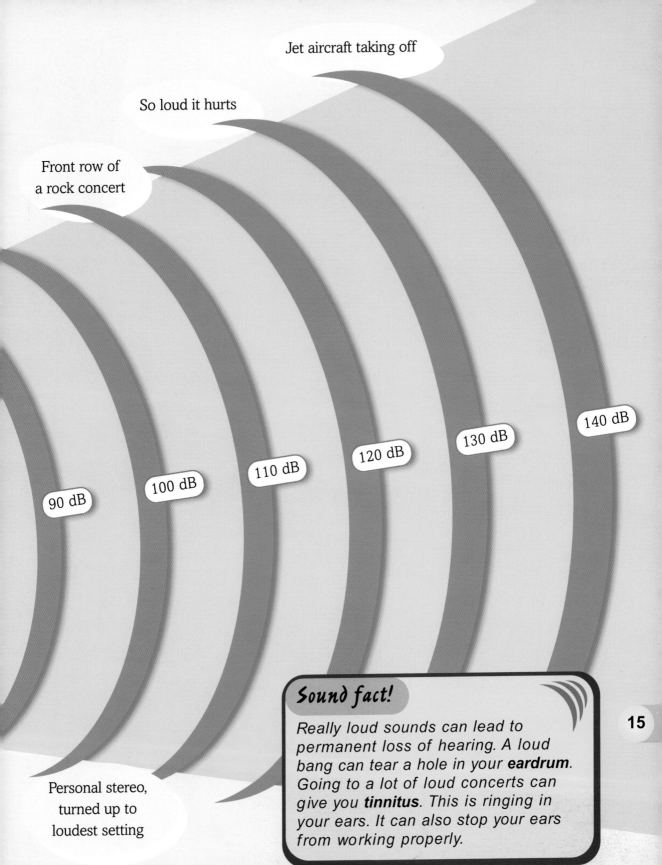

Sound fact!

Really loud sounds can lead to permanent loss of hearing. A loud bang can tear a hole in your **eardrum**. Going to a lot of loud concerts can give you **tinnitus**. This is ringing in your ears. It can also stop your ears from working properly.

Hit single

The band is half way through the show. They decide to play their latest hit single. The fans know the song. They go wild!

A tune or song is a sequence of different notes. The difference between notes is called **pitch**. Pitch means how high or low a sound is. The pitch depends on how fast a sound **vibrates**. The faster the **vibration**, the higher the pitch. The slower the vibration, the lower the pitch.

You use the keys or strings of an instrument to make different notes. When a guitarist presses a guitar string, it makes the string shorter. The note that comes out is higher.

When a string is longer, ▶
it vibrates more slowly.
This makes a lower
note.

◀When a string is
shorter, it vibrates
faster. This makes a
higher note.

17

So, why do
different instruments
sound different?

Making music

Why does the band sound so good together?

Each instrument has its own special sound. Why? Because it makes its own patterns of **sound waves**. These patterns depend on the shape of the instrument and what it is made of. So you can tell a trumpet from a guitar just by hearing them, even if they are playing the same note.

The sound waves of all the different instruments join together to make a song.

These graphs ▶ show the sound wave patterns each instrument makes. ▼

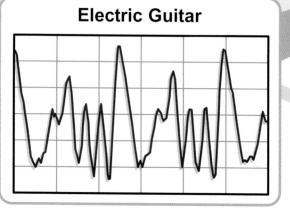

Electric Guitar

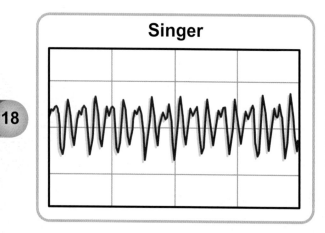

Singer

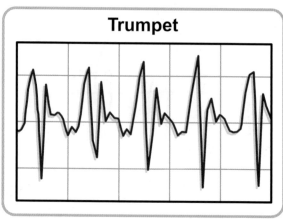

Trumpet

▲ A guitar works by making strings **vibrate** to make a sound.

You play a trumpet by making▼ your lips vibrate into it.

19

What about the singer?

The big chorus

The singer belts out the song at the top of her voice. The fans are singing along too.

The human voice is like an instrument. It changes **pitch** to make different high and low notes. Inside your throat are muscles called **vocal cords**. Your breath blowing past them makes them **vibrate**.

For higher notes, your throat makes your vocal cords shorter, so they vibrate faster. For lower notes, the vocal cords get longer. This means they vibrate more slowly.

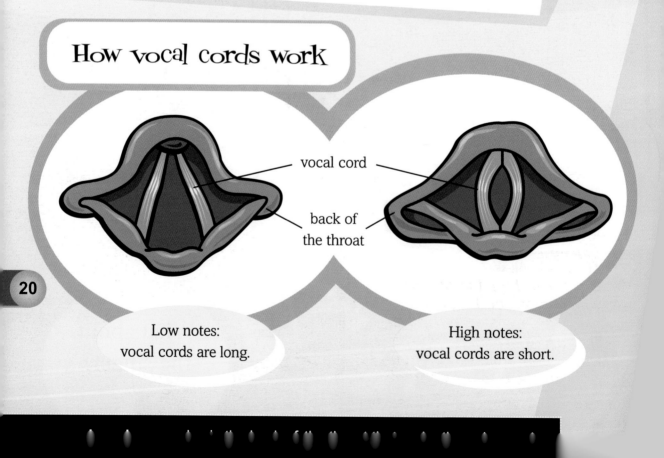

How vocal cords work

vocal cord

back of the throat

Low notes: vocal cords are long.

High notes: vocal cords are short.

The singer is often ▶ the most important person in a band. The singer sings the words and the main tune.

Sound fact!

Changing the pitch of your voice helps you to get your message across when you talk. Try saying "Yeah!" in an excited way and in a bored way. You use pitch to make them different.

21

How does hearing work?

➡

Sounds good

The band sounds better than ever! But how do you know what sounds good or bad? It is because of the way your ears and brain work together to help you hear.

The outer part of your ear catches sound **vibrations** in the air. The vibrations travel up a tube called the **ear canal.** Then they hit your **eardrum**.

From there, the vibrations travel into a snail-shaped, bony area. This is called the **cochlea**. The cochlea turns the vibrations into sound signals. The sound signals travel to your brain. Then, your brain works out what you are hearing.

Sound fact!

Many animals can hear better than humans. Scientists think dolphins may have the best hearing of all.

22

cochlea	snail-shaped part inside the ear
ear canal	hole leading into the ear

How you hear sounds

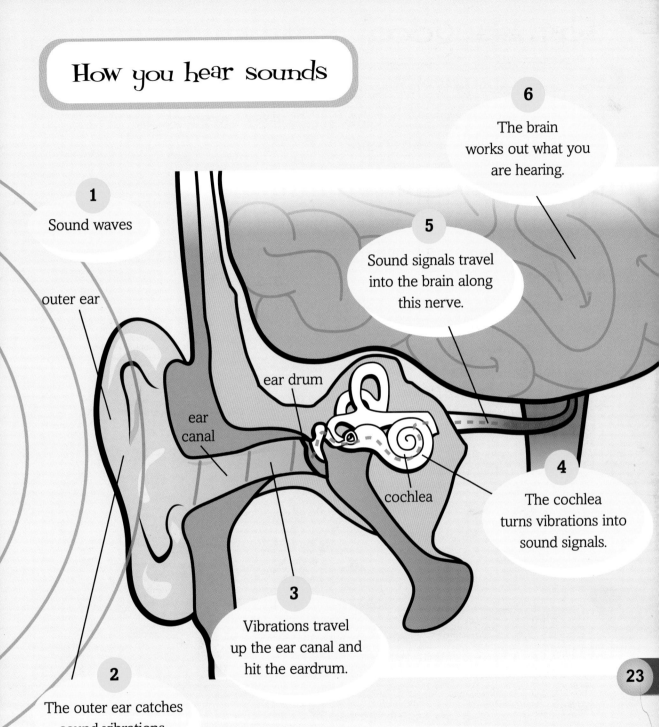

1 Sound waves

6 The brain works out what you are hearing.

5 Sound signals travel into the brain along this nerve.

outer ear

ear drum

ear canal

cochlea

4 The cochlea turns vibrations into sound signals.

3 Vibrations travel up the ear canal and hit the eardrum.

2 The outer ear catches sound vibrations.

23

The speed of sound

The band is playing the last song. Everyone in the area can hear it. But did you know that the further away the people are, the later they hear the sound?

If you were in the flats just outside the stadium, you would hear the sound about a second after the band played it. If you were 1 kilometre (0.6 miles) away, you would hear the sound 3 seconds later. This is because **sound waves** take almost 3 seconds to travel 1 kilometre (0.6 miles).

The people in the front row hear the sound straight away.

The people in the street outside the stadium hear the sound a second later.

supersonic   faster than the speed of sound

Sound fact!

If you watch a ball game from a distance, you often hear the sound a moment after you see the bat hit the ball. That is because it takes the sound a while to zoom through the air and reach your ears.

▲ Some planes are **supersonic**. That means they can go faster than the speed of sound.

World of sound

The show is over. The music stops. The fans leave. But there are still sounds everywhere – the sounds of everyday life.

Stop what you are doing right now, and you will hear those sounds. You might hear traffic or the hum of a computer. Perhaps you can hear someone coughing, or just your own breathing.

There is hardly a moment in your life when you can hear absolutely nothing. Many sounds, like a phone ringing or a fire alarm, can be really useful.

Just think how different life would be without sound …

As people leave the concert, there are many noises in the street outside. We are so used to these everyday noises that we ◀ hardly notice them.

Sound fact!

A composer called John Cage wrote a piece of music called 4'33". It is just 4 minutes, 33 seconds of silence! Cage wanted people to listen to the everyday sounds around them when the piece was performed.

Sound facts

Remember that loudness is measured in **decibels** (dB).
For every 10 decibels you go up, sound gets ten
times as loud. So a 50 decibels sound is 10
times louder than a 40 decibels sound.

The sound in the front row of a rock concert would measure 110 decibels.

10 dB 20 dB 30 dB 40 dB 50 dB 60 dB 70 dB 80 dB 90 dB 100 dB 110 dB

Normal talking measures 50 decibels.

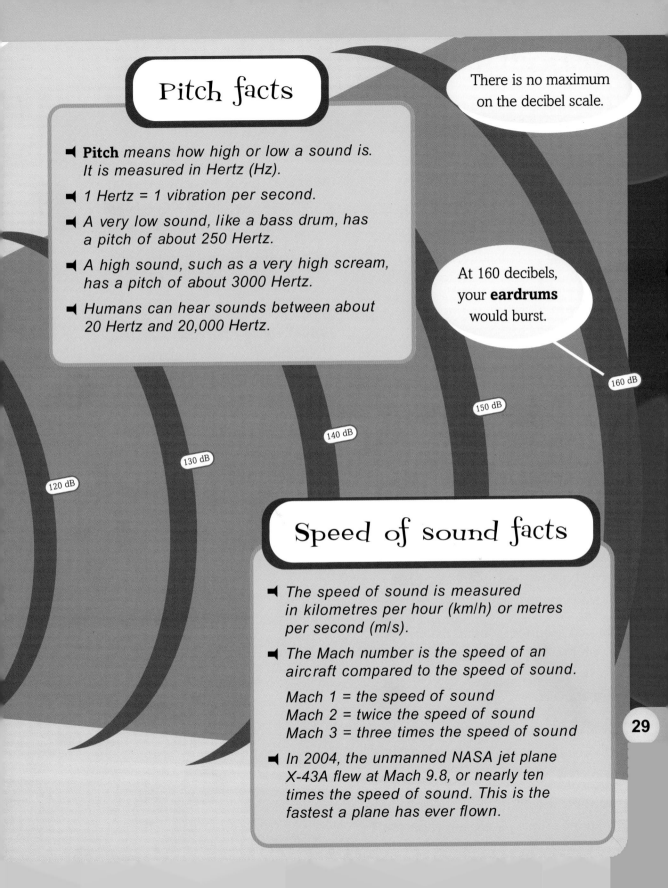

Pitch facts

- **Pitch** means how high or low a sound is. It is measured in Hertz (Hz).
- 1 Hertz = 1 vibration per second.
- A very low sound, like a bass drum, has a pitch of about 250 Hertz.
- A high sound, such as a very high scream, has a pitch of about 3000 Hertz.
- Humans can hear sounds between about 20 Hertz and 20,000 Hertz.

At 160 decibels, your **eardrums** would burst.

160 dB

150 dB

140 dB

130 dB

120 dB

Speed of sound facts

- The speed of sound is measured in kilometres per hour (km/h) or metres per second (m/s).
- The Mach number is the speed of an aircraft compared to the speed of sound.

  Mach 1 = the speed of sound
  Mach 2 = twice the speed of sound
  Mach 3 = three times the speed of sound

- In 2004, the unmanned NASA jet plane X-43A flew at Mach 9.8, or nearly ten times the speed of sound. This is the fastest a plane has ever flown.

29

Glossary

cochlea snail-shaped part inside the ear. The cochlea changes sound vibrations into nerve signals.

decibel (dB) measurement of loudness. A loud rock concert measures about 110 decibels.

ear canal hole leading into the ear. Sound travels along it to the eardrum.

eardrum thin skin in the ear that vibrates when sounds reach it. Very loud sounds can break your eardrum.

energy something we use to do work. Electricity, movement, and sound are all forms of energy.

percussion instruments you play by hitting them. Percussion instruments include drums, cowbells, and xylophones.

pitch how high or low a sound is. A "high-pitched" voice is a high, squeaky voice.

sound engineer sound expert who makes sure bands sound good. He or she checks the sound before a concert.

sound waves sound vibrations moving through air. Unlike ocean waves, they are invisible.

supersonic faster than the speed of sound. Some planes are supersonic.

tinnitus ringing or buzzing sound in the ears. It can be caused by hearing too many loud noises.

vibrate to move backwards and forwards quickly. A guitar string vibrates when you pluck it.

vibrations fast backwards and forwards movements. All sounds are caused by vibrations.

vocal cords muscles in the back of the throat that make the voice work. You blow air past them to make a noise.

Want to know more?

Books to read

- *Horrible Science: Sounds Dreadful,* by Nick Arnold (Scholastic, 1998)
- *Learn to Play: Drums,* by E. O'Brien (Usborne, 1998)
- *Learn to Play: Electric Guitar,* by Anthony Marks (Usborne, 1995)
- *Pop World: Pop Concerts,* by Kay Rowley (Hodder Wayland, 1991)

Places to visit

- The Musical Museum
  368 High Street
  Brentford
  Middlesex TW8 0BD
  United Kingdom

- Science Museum
  Exhibition Road
  London SW7 2DD
  United Kingdom
  www.sciencemuseum.org.uk

Like sound, light is a useful form of energy. Find out all about it in ***Voyage of a Light Beam***.

Check out ***Wackiest Machines Ever!*** to find out how one form of energy can change into another.

Index